W9-CDA-264

The

Watercolor
PAINTER'S
POCKET
PALETTE

Instant, practical visual guidance

on mixing and matching

watercolors to suit all subjects.

Moira Clinch

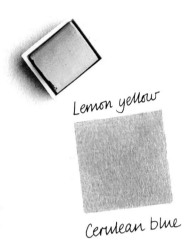

Lemon yellow

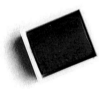

Cerulean blue

NORTH LIGHT BOOKS
Cincinnati, Ohio

A QUARTO BOOK

First published in the U.S.A. by North Light Books, an imprint of F & W Publications, Inc, 1507 Dana Avenue, Cincinnati, Ohio 45207

First published 1991
Reprinted 1992, 1993
Reprinted 1994

Copyright © 1991
Quarto Publishing plc

ISBN 0-89134-401-2

Reprinted 1995

All rights reserved
No part of this publication may be reproduced, stored in a retrieval system or transmitted in any form or by any means electronic, mechanical, photocopying, recording or otherwise, without the prior permission of the publisher.

This book was designed and produced by Quarto Publishing plc The Old Brewery 6 Blundell Street London N7 9BH

While every care has been taken with the printing of the color charts, the publishers cannot guarantee total accuracy in every case.

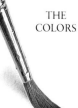

THE
COLORS

page 10
Cerulean blue

page 11
Cobalt blue

page 12
French ultramarine

page 18
Terre verte

page 19
Viridian

page 20
Sap green

page 21
Hooker's green dark

page 29
Naples yellow

page 30
Yellow ochre

page 31
Cadmium orange

page 36
Bright red

page 40
Rose doré

page 41
Permanent rose

page 44
Cobalt violet

page 45
Winsor violet

page 51
Venetian red

page 52
Burnt umber

page 53
Sepia

page 56
Payne's gray

page **13**
Winsor blue

page **14**
Prussian blue

page **15**
Indigo

page **26**
Lemon yellow

page **27**
Aureolin

page **28**
Cadmium
yellow

page **37**
Cadmium red

page **38**
Alizarin
crimson

page **39**
Rose madder
genuine

page **48**
Raw sienna

page **49**
Raw umber

page **50**
Burnt sienna

page **57**
Davy's gray

page **60**
Ivory black

page **61**
Chinese white

Contents

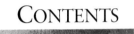

USING THIS BOOK   **4**

USING SKY BLUES   **16**
Bosham Clouds

MIXING GREENS   **22**

USING AND MIXING
GREENS   **24**
Rydal Water

MIXING ORANGES   **32**

YELLOWS AND REDS   **34**
Flowers for Emily

MIXING WARM
PIGMENTS   **42**
La Bougainvillea

MIXING PURPLES   **46**

USING BROWNS AND
BLUES   **54**
Red Flag Markers, Whitby

MUTED COLORS   **58**
Fen Cottage

USEFUL MIXES: SKIN   **62**

Credits   **64**

USING THIS BOOK

THE PURPOSE OF THIS BOOK is to provide the watercolor artist with an at-a-glance guide to over 800 mixes and overpainting effects. More experienced watercolorists will already know their favorite color combinations, but hopefully this book will yield some surprises, even in the case of colors that the artist uses regularly. The beginner can cut out trial and error time by selecting a possible basic palette to work with.

Most artists tend to work with a limited number (approximately 12) of colors, known as a basic palette. The choice of colors is a matter of personal preference, but since paint manufacturers produce a vast number it can sometimes be confusing. *The Painter's Pocket Palette* helps not only in the selection of colors but also more creatively, by exploring the possibility of adding a new and hith-

Each page features one of the 34 chosen colors in various permutations. This is referred to as the main color (1). For a visual guide to these colors see pages 2 and 3. Each main color is mixed with a constant basic palette (2), see opposite, which is repeated on every page. The main color is also shown as an area of dry flat wash with the same basic palette overpainted as brushstrokes on top of it (3). The symbols (4) denote various characteristics of the main color (see page 9).

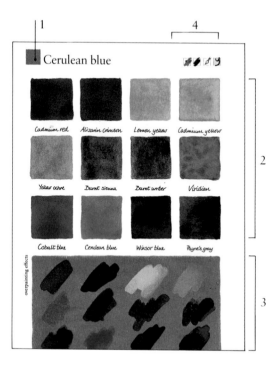

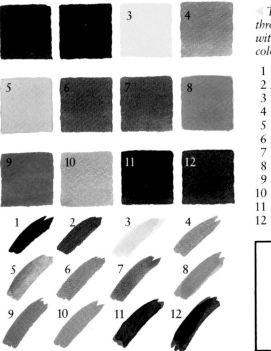

This is the basic palette used throughout the book, shown here without the addition of the main color

1 *Cadmium red*
2 *Alizarin crimson*
3 *Lemon yellow*
4 *Cadmium yellow*
5 *Yellow ochre*
6 *Burnt sienna*
7 *Burnt umber*
8 *Viridian*
9 *Cobalt blue*
10 *Cerulean blue*
11 *Winsor blue*
12 *Payne's gray*

REMEMBER

*The main color is featured **once** on its own page. The basic palette repeats **twice** on every page.*

---

erto unknown color to your paintbox. The 34 colors chosen are the more familiar ones, and all are reliable and durable (see symbols p9).

How many times have you almost bought a new pigment, or actually bought it only to find yourself reverting to the old safe, familiar mixes? The page-by-page chart layout of the book provides accessible and easy-to-compare visual information, so that using new colors ceases to be an alarming and hit-and-miss affair and becomes an exciting and creative one. You can see at a glance how to achieve the color mix you want, and just as importantly you can see when a mix is not appropriate for a particular effect.

THE BASIC PALETTE

The basic palette chosen for the book is shown above, but this is only a suggested starting point; you may add or replace colors as you choose. For example, you may prefer to use French ultramarine instead of Winsor blue as part of your own selection.

5

MIXING SECONDARY COLORS

The secondary colors, green, orange and purple, can be bought as various hues in tube or pan form, but generally more colors can be achieved — and it is more fun — if you mix your own.

These pages show how by mixing two primaries together, or by mixing a primary with one of the proprietary secondaries, such as sap green or one of the purples, you can create both intense and muted secondaries. An extra feature is a graduated color strip showing degrees of mixing the two colors.

There are some secondary hues, however, such as viridian and cadmium orange, which cannot be mixed from two primaries as they have an intensity which it is impossible to reproduce.

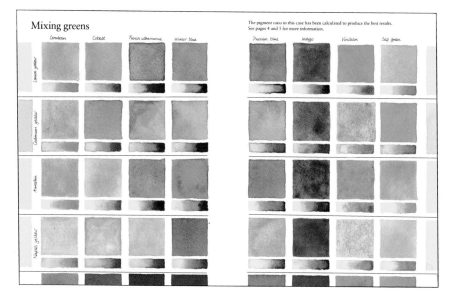

This page showing secondary color mixing is repeated three times in the book to show various mixes of green, orange and purple.

UNDERSTANDING THE MIXTURES

When mixing secondaries, you will need to know which of the primaries to use, as there are many versions of each one. As you can see from the color wheel, each one has a bias toward another, for instance cadmium red veers toward yellow, so it makes sense when trying to achieve an intense secondary to exploit this bias.

Conversely, if you want to mix a neutral secondary or neutral colors, mixing colors that contain the opposite or complementary color on the color wheel will give a muted or even muddy result.

▶ When colors are placed next to one another you can see the color bias clearly.

▼ These charts show how the choice of the primary color affects the mixture. Those closest together on the wheel create intense secondaries, while those furthest apart create neutrals.

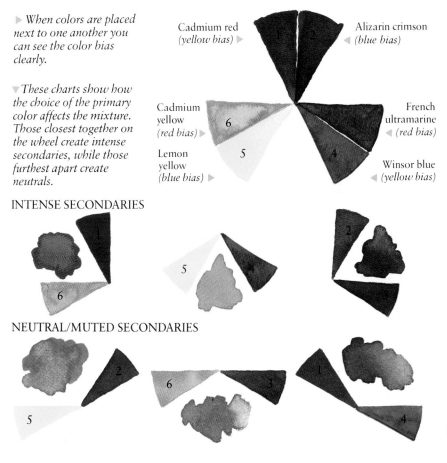

Cadmium red
(yellow bias) ▶

Alizarin crimson
◀ *(blue bias)*

Cadmium yellow
(red bias) ▶

French ultramarine
◀ *(red bias)*

Lemon yellow
(blue bias) ▶

Winsor blue
◀ *(yellow bias)*

INTENSE SECONDARIES

NEUTRAL/MUTED SECONDARIES

UNDERSTANDING THE SYMBOLS

Every watercolor pigment has its own characteristics, and all the colors shown in this book have been coded to help you identify at a glance the different properties.

Transparency
One of the most exciting, if unpredictable, qualities of watercolor is its ability to impart color while allowing underlying layers to remain visible to a greater or lesser degree. Linked to this is the way in which pigments can be diluted with water so that the white of the paper itself dilutes the color, rather than "polluting" the color with white, as is the case with opaque paints. Because of the transparency of watercolor, the usual way of working is from light to dark, gradually building up layers. Transparency, however, is relative, and because some pigments are considerably more opaque than others they are categorized as transparent, semi-transparent and opaque.

The amount of water used is a matter of personal preference, but generally a

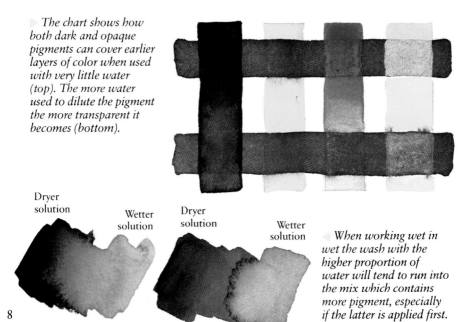

The chart shows how both dark and opaque pigments can cover earlier layers of color when used with very little water (top). The more water used to dilute the pigment the more transparent it becomes (bottom).

Dryer
solution

Wetter
solution

Dryer
solution

Wetter
solution

When working wet in wet the wash with the higher proportion of water will tend to run into the mix which contains more pigment, especially if the latter is applied first.

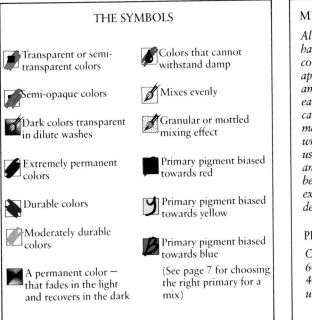

THE SYMBOLS

Transparent or semi-transparent colors

Semi-opaque colors

Dark colors transparent in dilute washes

Extremely permanent colors

Durable colors

Moderately durable colors

A permanent color — that fades in the light and recovers in the dark

Colors that cannot withstand damp

Mixes evenly

Granular or mottled mixing effect

Primary pigment biased towards red

Primary pigment biased towards yellow

Primary pigment biased towards blue

(See page 7 for choosing the right primary for a mix)

MIXES IN THIS BOOK

All the colors in this book have been mixed under control conditions, with approximately the same amount of water used for each one. This has been calculated to create a medium-strength mix, which provides the most useful guidance. Stronger and weaker amounts can be visualized and experimented with if desired.

PIGMENT RATIO

On main color pages:
60% main color
40% basic palette color
unless stated otherwise

tighter more detailed style uses a higher mix of pigment to water than a looser one. As a rule the more water used the more unpredictable the result. No two mixes will ever contain the same amount of water, and the solution with the higher percentage of water will "run" into the less diluted mix. This "pushes" the pigment, creating intriguing, if unpredictable, effects. Tanalizingly, it is seldom possible to recreate them, as they are never exactly the same.

Permanence
Watercolors are graded for permanence, the main categories being extremely permanent, durable, moderately durable and fugitive. Some colors which are durable in strong washes are less durable when applied in thin washes, and other colors fluctuate; they fade in sunlight and recover in the dark.

Mixing qualities
Some pigments mix very evenly while others mix creating granular or interesting mottled effects.

9

Cerulean blue

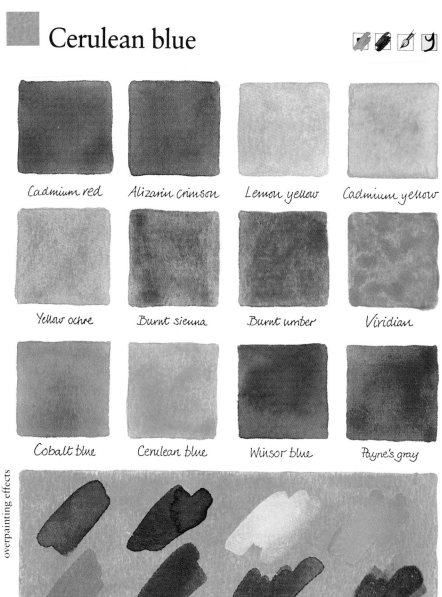

Cadmium red

Alizarin crimson

Lemon yellow

Cadmium yellow

Yellow ochre

Burnt sienna

Burnt umber

Viridian

Cobalt blue

Cerulean blue

Winsor blue

Payne's gray

10

Cobalt blue

Cadmium red	Alizarin Crimson	Lemon yellow	Cadmium yellow
Yellow ochre	Burnt sienna	Burnt umber	Viridian
Cobalt blue	Cerulean blue	Winsor blue	Payne's gray

overpainting effects

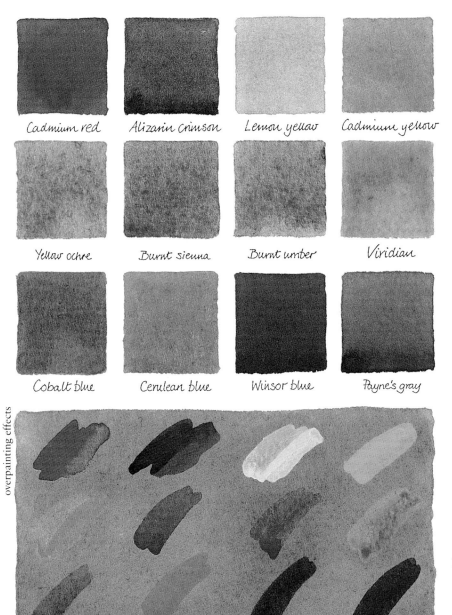

11

French ultramarine

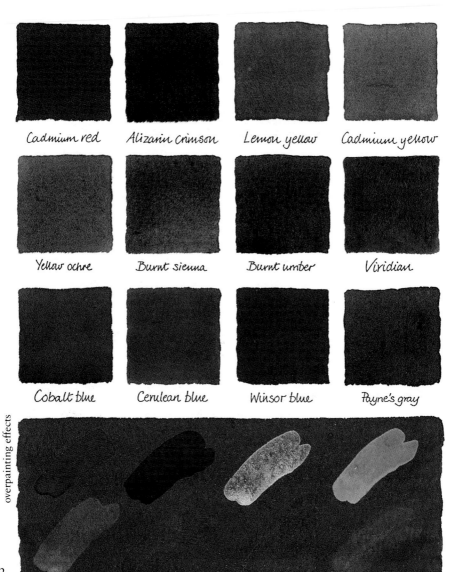

Cadmium red   Alizarin crimson   Lemon yellow   Cadmium yellow

Yellow ochre   Burnt sienna   Burnt umber   Viridian

Cobalt blue   Cerulean blue   Winsor blue   Payne's gray

overpainting effects

Winsor blue

Cadmium red	Alizarin crimson
Lemon yellow	Cadmium yellow

Yellow ochre	Burnt sienna
Burnt umber	Viridian

Cobalt blue	Cerulean blue
Winsor blue	Payne's gray

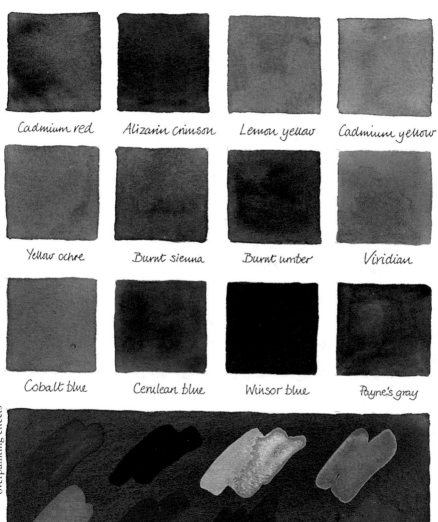

overpainting effects

13

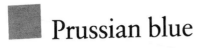 # Prussian blue

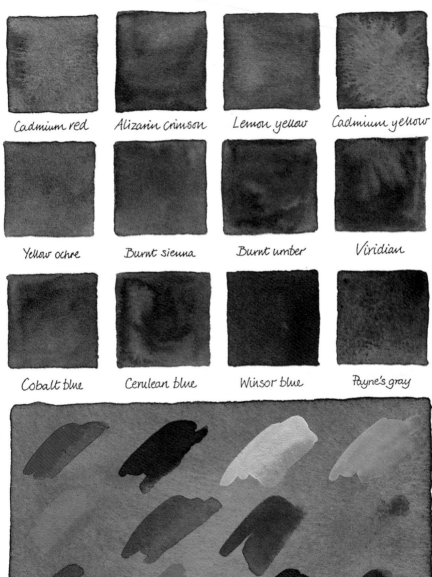

Cadmium red	Alizarin crimson	Lemon yellow	Cadmium yellow
Yellow ochre	Burnt sienna	Burnt umber	Viridian
Cobalt blue	Cerulean blue	Winsor blue	Payne's gray

overpainting effects

14

Indigo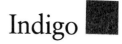

Cadmium red	Alizarin crimson	Lemon yellow	Cadmium yellow
Yellow ochre	Burnt sienna	Burnt umber	Viridian
Cobalt blue	Cerulean blue	Winsor blue	Payne's gray

overpainting effects

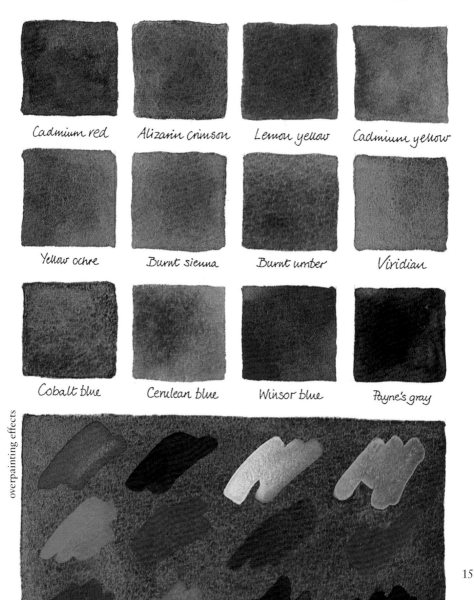

15

USING SKY BLUES

Bosham Clouds
7ins × 10ins

THE BLUE PIGMENT chosen to represent the sky is a matter of personal preference, but generally the blues which are biased toward yellow give the effect of sunlight, and when strongly diluted with water look warm and hazy. Paradoxically, those containing traces of red can seem cooler, and when applied as a thin wash create a crisp effect.

To capture the fluidity of cloud formations the artist needs to analyse the values and shapes very quickly, and then to simplify them. Highlights, wispy clouds or the tops of "cotton wool" clouds tops are usually left as white paper. The mid-tones and the dark undersides can be proprietary gray watercolors or pigments such as ultramarine and cadmium red mixed with touches of other colors for variety.

▶ *The blue sky was a medium to weak dilution of ultramarine, with the contrast between wet, uneven washes and areas of dry brushwork giving life to this single pigment. In general, blue sky colors are better unmixed unless painting sunrises or sunsets.*

◀ *Gray cloud areas were achieved by various mixtures of ultramarine and touches of cadmium red, the latter giving subtle warmth and interest to the gray, while rapid streaking brushstrokes were used for the dark undersides of the clouds.*

ARTIST Christopher Baker

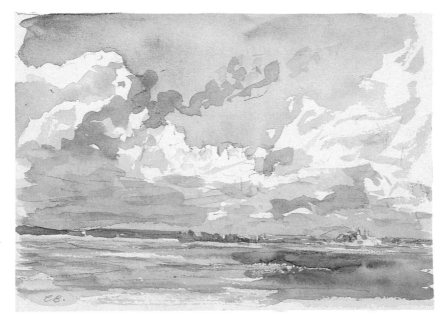

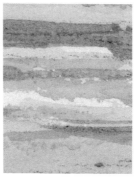

◀ *The flat foreground landscape has sunlit patches of yellow ochre, areas of muted viridian, and for the far distance touches of ultramarine.*

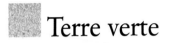 # Terre verte

Cadmium red	Alizarin crimson
Lemon yellow	Cadmium yellow
Yellow ochre	Burnt sienna
Burnt umber	Viridian
Cobalt blue	Cerulean blue
Winsor blue	Payne's gray

overpainting effects

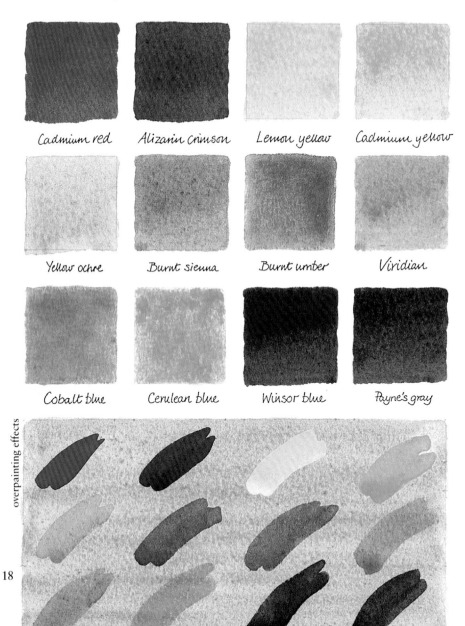

18

Viridian

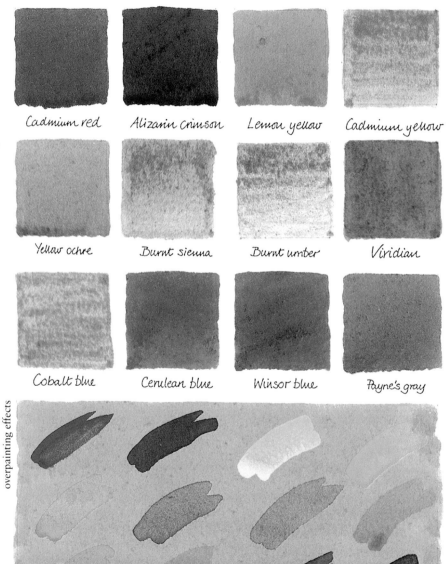

Cadmium red	Alizarin crimson	Lemon yellow	Cadmium yellow
Yellow ochre	Burnt sienna	Burnt umber	Viridian
Cobalt blue	Cerulean blue	Winsor blue	Payne's gray

overpainting effects

19

Sap green

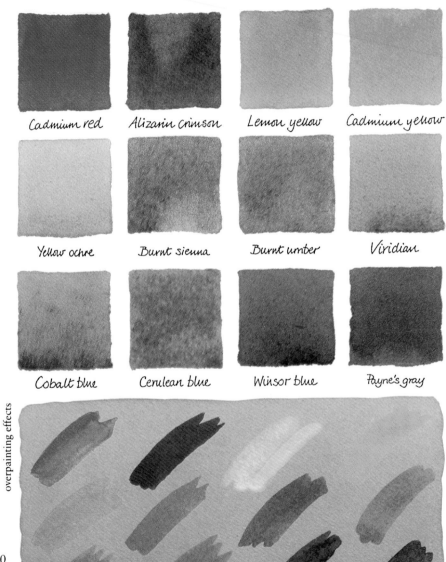

Cadmium red	Alizarin crimson	Lemon yellow	Cadmium yellow
Yellow ochre	Burnt sienna	Burnt umber	Viridian
Cobalt blue	Cerulean blue	Winsor blue	Payne's gray

overpainting effects

20

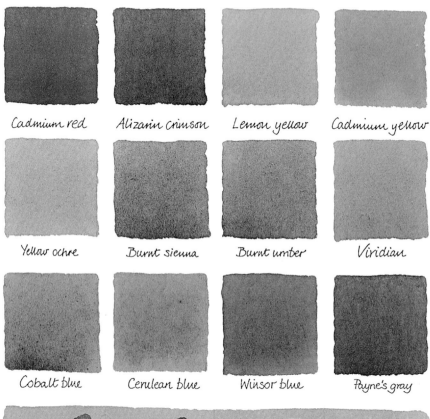

Cadmium red	Alizarin crimson	Lemon yellow	Cadmium yellow
Yellow ochre	Burnt sienna	Burnt umber	Viridian
Cobalt blue	Cerulean blue	Winsor blue	Payne's gray

overpainting effects

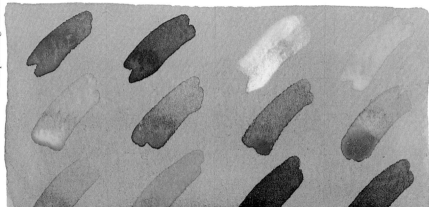

Mixing greens

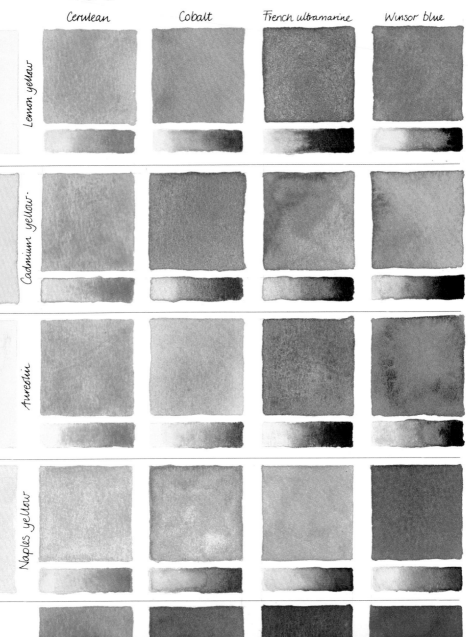

Cerulean   Cobalt   French ultramarine   Winsor blue

Lemon yellow

Cadmium yellow

Aureolin

Naples yellow

The pigment ratio in this case has been calculated to produce the best results.
See pages 4 and 5 for more information.

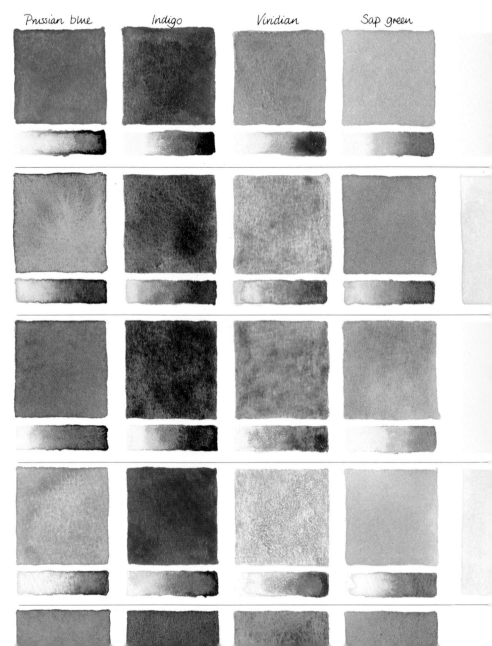

Prussian blue   Indigo   Viridian   Sap green

USING AND MIXING GREENS

Rydal Water
15ins × 23ins

TO CREATE the effect of a landscape bathed in sunlight the artist used yellow ochre, cadmium yellow and lemon yellow as the basis of this painting. These colors were mixed with cobalt blue, Prussian blue, indigo and Paynes gray to create the various green hues. Most colors were mixed on a palette, but in some areas thin washes of color were overpainted on dry base colors to achieve variety, and some shadow areas were applied wet in wet so that they mixed on the paper.

▶ *The detailed leaf areas were gradually built up from a wash of yellow ochre with three subsequent layers of a Prussian blue and cadmium yellow mix.*

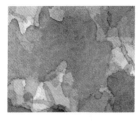

▲ *The blue of the sky was a simple, unevenly applied wash of cerulean blue, and the clouds thin mixes of Paynes gray and touches of lamp black. The billowing white cloud edges were achieved by leaving areas of the paper unpainted, as this produces a clearer, purer white than opaque white paint.*

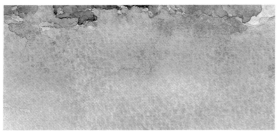

▲ *Yellow ochre was used as the first wash for the fields and trees in all the foreground areas. This gives warmth to the painting and accords with the colors of late summer.*

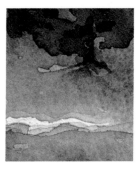

◀ *The shadow area was created by a thin wash of Paynes gray and indigo.*

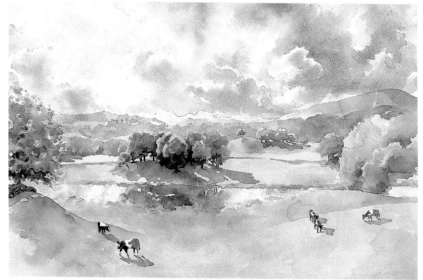

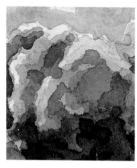

◀ *The trees are in effect backlit, as the direction of the sun is just off to the left of the picture area. The strong highlights on the edges of the trees were particularly important in conveying this, so base washes of lemon yellow were left untouched, and dark shadow areas built up to contrast with them.*

Lemon yellow

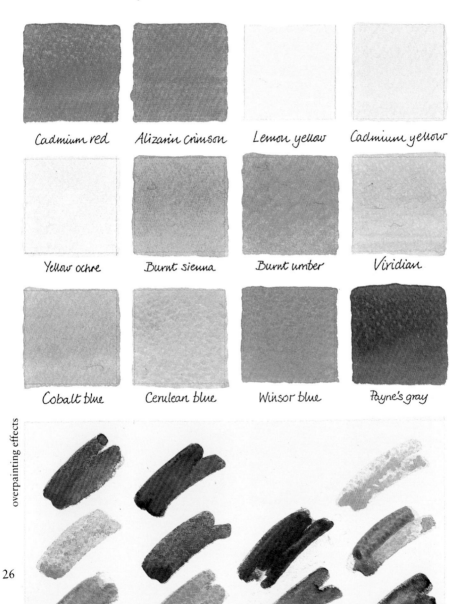

Cadmium red	Alizarin crimson
Lemon yellow	Cadmium yellow
Yellow ochre	Burnt sienna
Burnt umber	Viridian
Cobalt blue	Cerulean blue
Winsor blue	Payne's gray

overpainting effects

26

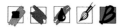

Aureolin

Cadmium red   Alizarin crimson   Lemon yellow   Cadmium yellow

Yellow ochre   Burnt sienna   Burnt umber   Viridian

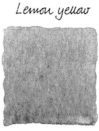 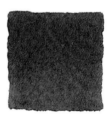

Cobalt blue   Cerulean blue   Winsor blue   Payne's gray

overpainting effects

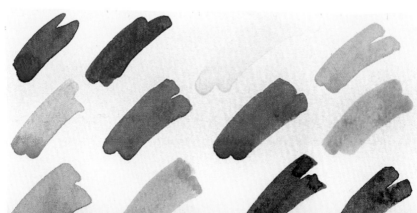

27

Cadmium yellow

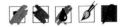

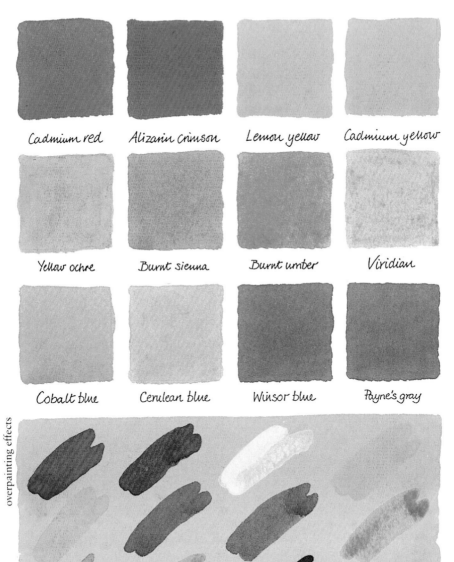

Cadmium red	Alizarin crimson
Lemon yellow	Cadmium yellow
Yellow ochre	Burnt sienna
Burnt umber	Viridian
Cobalt blue	Cerulean blue
Winsor blue	Payne's gray

overpainting effects

28

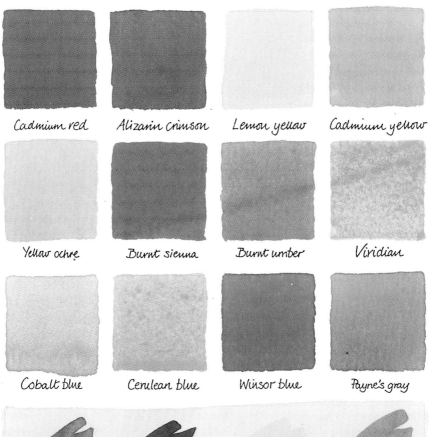

Cadmium red	Alizarin crimson
Lemon yellow	Cadmium yellow
Yellow ochre	Burnt sienna
Burnt umber	Viridian
Cobalt blue	Cerulean blue
Winsor blue	Payne's gray

overpainting effects

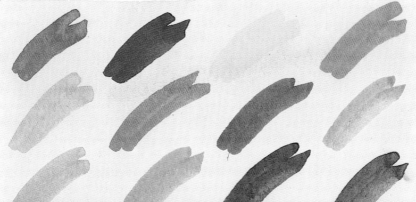

Yellow ochre

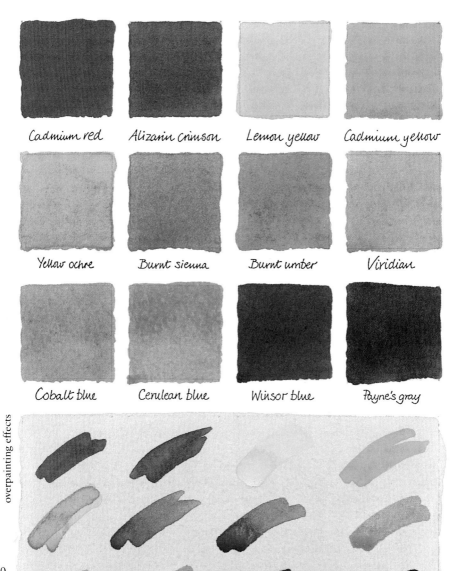

Cadmium red	Alizarin crimson	Lemon yellow	Cadmium yellow
Yellow ochre	Burnt sienna	Burnt umber	Viridian
Cobalt blue	Cerulean blue	Winsor blue	Payne's gray

overpainting effects

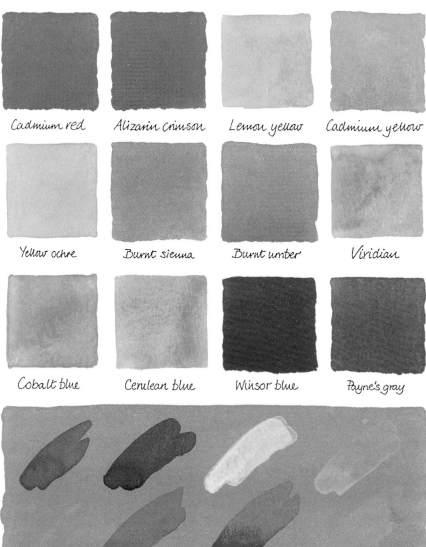

Cadmium red	Alizarin crimson	Lemon yellow	Cadmium yellow
Yellow ochre	Burnt sienna	Burnt umber	Viridian
Cobalt blue	Cerulean blue	Winsor blue	Payne's gray

overpainting effects

Mixing oranges

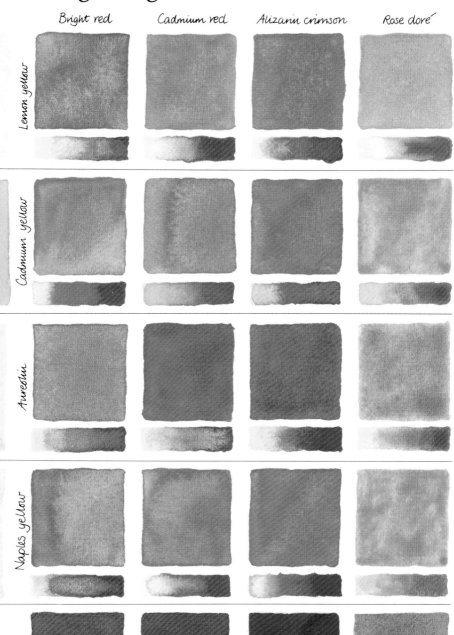

	Bright red	Cadmium red	Alizarin crimson	Rose doré
Lemon yellow				
Cadmium yellow				
Aureolin				
Naples yellow				

The pigment ratio in this case has been calculated to give the brightest oranges.
See pages 4 and 5 for more information.

Rose madder
genuine

Permanent rose

Burnt sienna

Cadmium orange

YELLOWS AND REDS

Flowers for Emily
11 ins × 7½ ins

THE FLICKERING PATTERN of pure white paper highlights in this painting conveys the impression of sunlight streaming in through the window. This warmth is further emphasized by the use of cadmium yellow in the various greens and the wet-in-wet additions of alizarin crimson even in the "cool" shadow areas. The strong foreground shadow stabilizes the composition and contrasts with the flowers and the background window to emphasize the sunlit effect.

▶ *The green hues were various mixes of Prussian blue, indigo and cadmium yellow. To create both the pale greens of the background and the stronger greens of the foliage, the colors were mixed in different proportions and with varying amounts of water.*

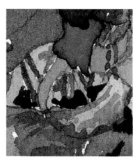

▽ *Several subtle mixes were used for the yellow roses, the first being a very thin dilution of cadmium yellow. The darker layers were strong mixes of cadmium yellow with small amounts of cadmium red and Paynes gray.*

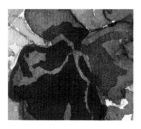

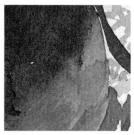

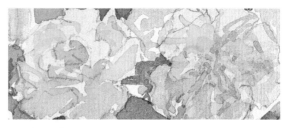

▲ *The red rose was begun with a flat underwash of cadmium red. The darker details of the petals were then painted with a strong mixture of cadmium red, alizarin crimson and a touch of indigo.*

◀ *The strong foreground shadow is a mixture of indigo with cadmium red and alizarin crimson, the two red pigments giving a touch of warmth which echoes the color of the roses.*

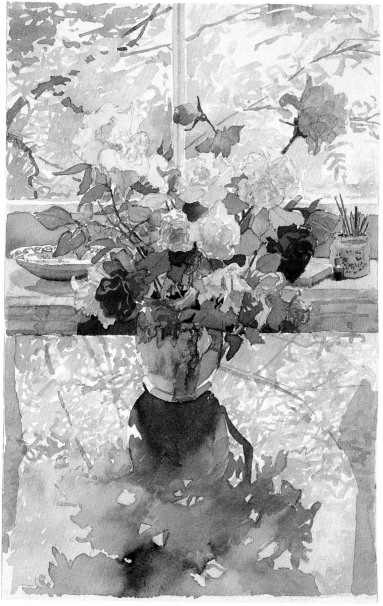

ARTIST Annie Williams

35

Bright red

Cadmium red

Alizarin crimson

Lemon yellow

Cadmium yellow

Yellow ochre

Burnt sienna *

Burnt umber

Viridian

Cobalt blue

Cerulean blue

Winsor blue

Payne's gray

overpainting effects

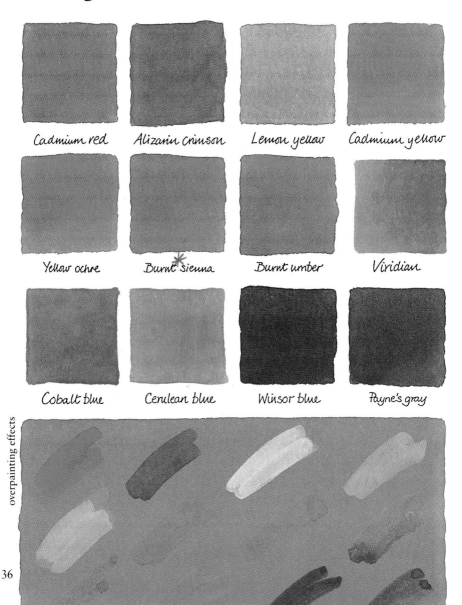

36

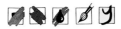

Cadmium red

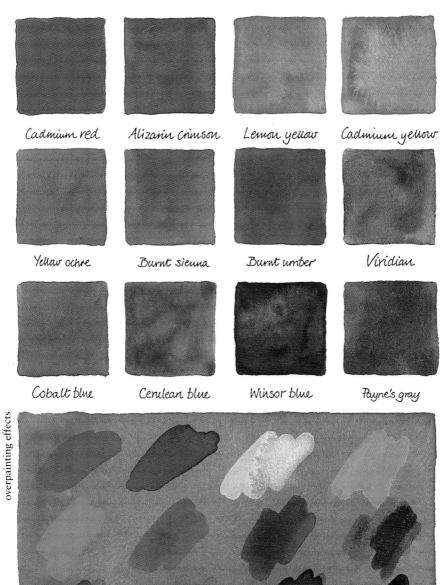

Cadmium red

Alizarin crimson

Lemon yellow

Cadmium yellow

Yellow ochre

Burnt sienna

Burnt umber

Viridian

Cobalt blue

Cerulean blue

Winsor blue

Payne's gray

overpainting effects

37

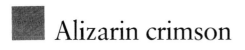 # Alizarin crimson

Cadmium red	Alizarin crimson	Lemon yellow	Cadmium yellow
Yellow ochre	Burnt sienna	Burnt umber	Viridian
Cobalt blue	Cerulean blue	Winsor blue	Payne's gray

overpainting effects

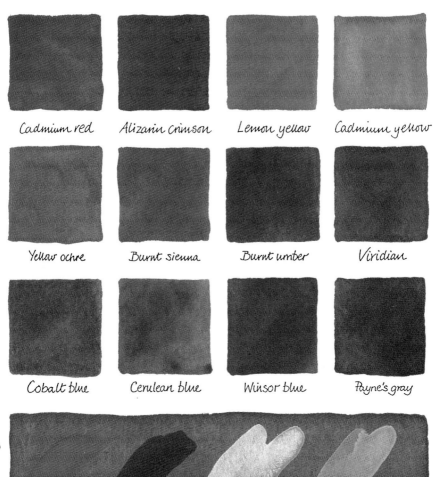

38

Rose madder genuine

Cadmium red	Alizarin crimson	Lemon yellow	Cadmium yellow
Yellow ochre	Burnt sienna	Burnt umber	Viridian
Cobalt blue	Cerulean blue	Winsor blue	Payne's gray

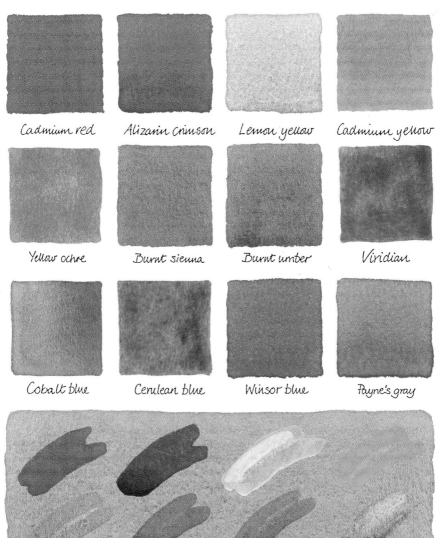

Rose doré

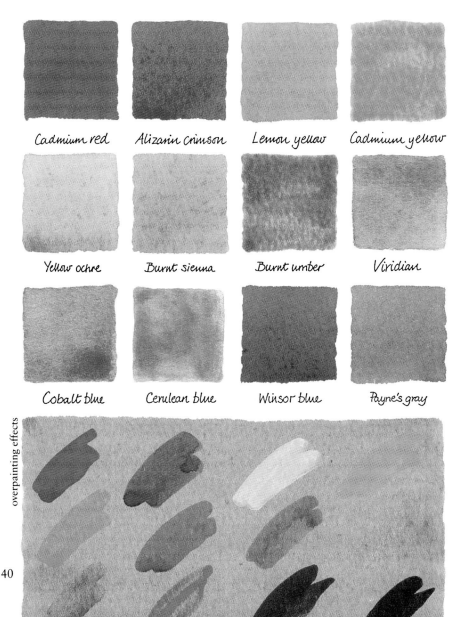

Cadmium red	Alizarin crimson
Lemon yellow	Cadmium yellow
Yellow ochre	Burnt sienna
Burnt umber	Viridian
Cobalt blue	Cerulean blue
Winsor blue	Payne's gray

overpainting effects

Permanent rose

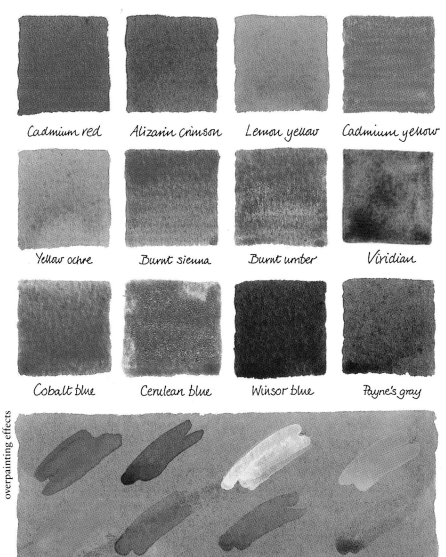

Cadmium red	Alizarin crimson	Lemon yellow	Cadmium yellow
Yellow ochre	Burnt sienna	Burnt umber	Viridian
Cobalt blue	Cerulean blue	Winsor blue	Payne's gray

overpainting effects

MIXING WARM PIGMENTS

La Bougainvillea
19ins × 13ins

THE WARM COLORS of burnt sienna, yellow ochre and burnt umber form the basis of this painting. The versatility of a single watercolor pigment is demonstrated by the fact that burnt umber was used to depict both the somber nature of the gate and the delicate plasterwork of the wall. The only difference between the two is the amount of water used to apply the paint.

▶ *A strongly diluted flat underwash of burnt sienna was used as the basis for the brickwork. Individual bricks were then overpainted in diluted mixtures of cadmium deep red, raw sienna and yellow ochre.*

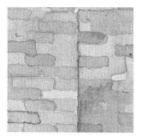

▼ *The highlights of the bougainvillea flowers were painted in concentrated rose madder carmine, while shadows were formed by subduing the color with indigo.*

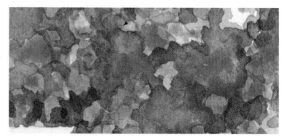

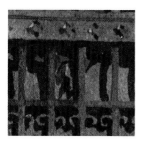

▲ *The iron gate was painted in a mixture of burnt umber and lamp black, with extra black and indigo for the shadow area.*

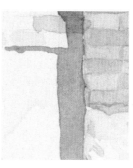

◀ *The shadow here was achieved by applying a medium dilution of Paynes gray over very thin dilutions of yellow ochre and raw sienna, and exceptionally thin washes of burnt umber.*

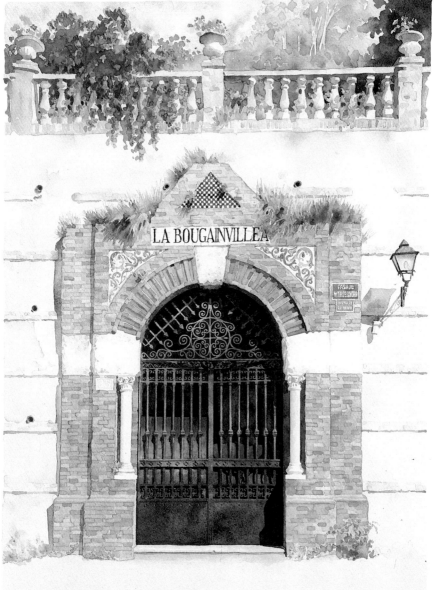

LA BOUGAINVILLEA

ARTIST Moira Clinch

43

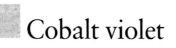 # Cobalt violet

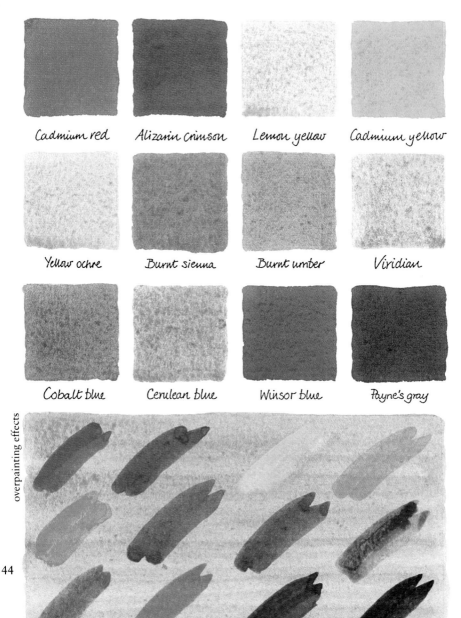

Cadmium red Alizarin crimson Lemon yellow Cadmium yellow

Yellow ochre Burnt sienna Burnt umber Viridian

Cobalt blue Cerulean blue Winsor blue Payne's gray

overpainting effects

Winsor violet

Cadmium red

Alizarin crimson

Lemon yellow

Cadmium yellow

Yellow ochre

Burnt sienna

Burnt umber

Viridian

Cobalt blue

Cerulean blue

Winsor blue

Payne's gray

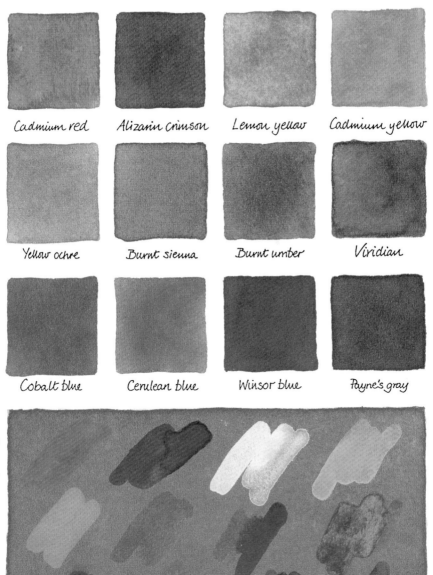

overpainting effects

45

Mixing purples

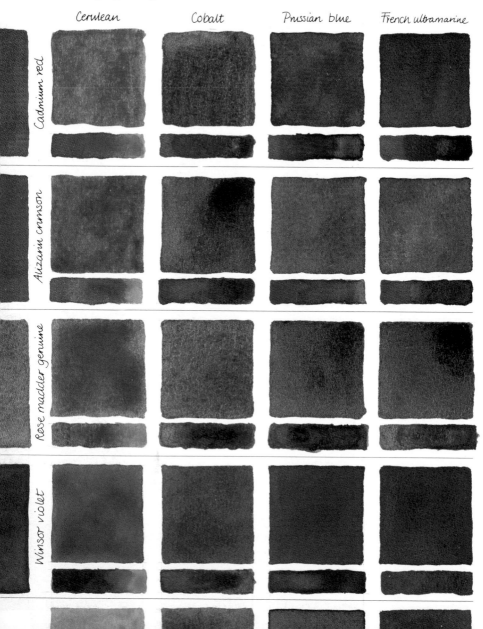

	Cerulean	Cobalt	Prussian blue	French ultramarine
Cadmium red				
Alizarin crimson				
Rose madder genuine				
Winsor violet				

The proportions of the pigment mixtures have been chosen to produce the most satisfactory purples. See pages 4 and 5 for more information.

Winsor blue   Indigo   Cobalt violet   Winsor violet

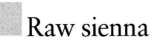 # Raw sienna

Cadmium red	Alizarin crimson	Lemon yellow	Cadmium yellow
Yellow ochre	Burnt sienna	Burnt umber	Viridian
Cobalt blue	Cerulean blue	Winsor blue	Payne's gray

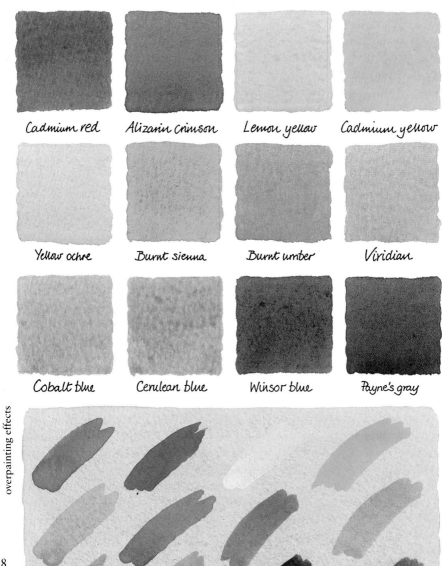

overpainting effects

48

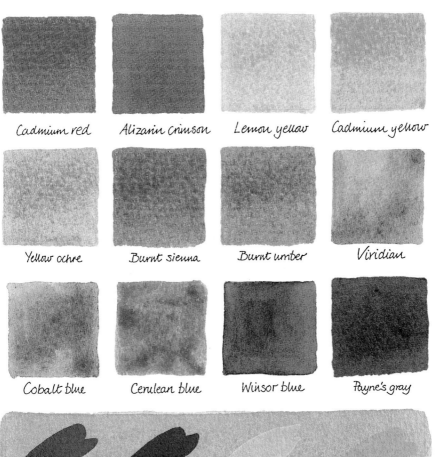

Cadmium red

Alizarin crimson

Lemon yellow

Cadmium yellow

Yellow ochre

Burnt sienna

Burnt umber

Viridian

Cobalt blue

Cerulean blue

Winsor blue

Payne's gray

overpainting effects

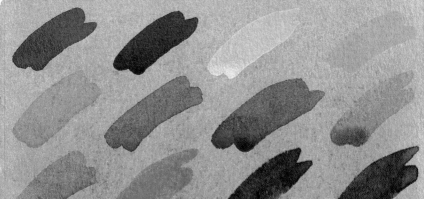

49

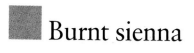 # Burnt sienna

Cadmium red	Alizarin crimson
Lemon yellow	Cadmium yellow

Cadmium red

Alizarin crimson

Lemon yellow

Cadmium yellow

Yellow ochre

Burnt sienna

Burnt umber

Viridian

Cobalt blue

Cerulean blue

Winsor blue

Payne's gray

overpainting effects

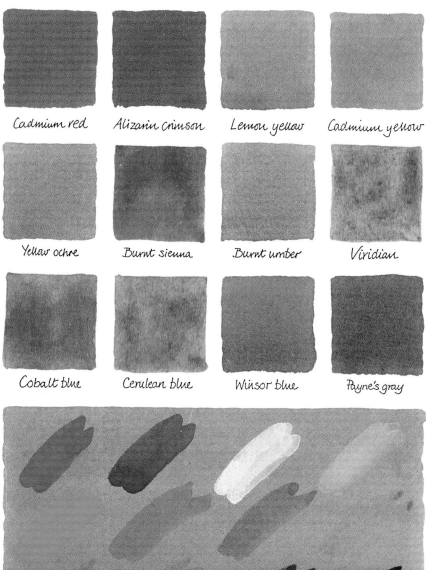

50

Venetian red

Cadmium red	Alizarin Crimson	Lemon yellow	Cadmium yellow
Yellow ochre	Burnt sienna	Burnt umber	Viridian
Cobalt blue	Cerulean blue	Winsor blue	Payne's gray

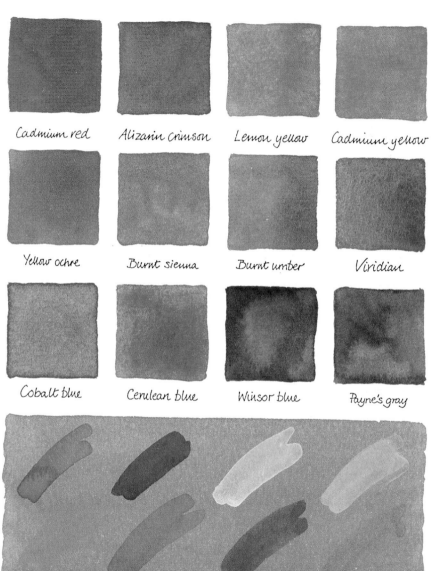

Burnt umber

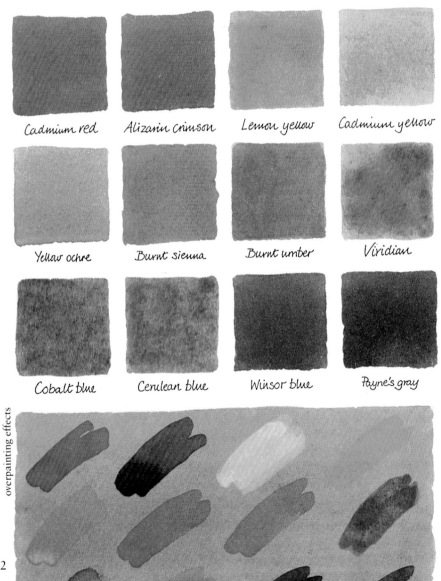

Cadmium red	Alizarin crimson	Lemon yellow	Cadmium yellow
Yellow ochre	Burnt sienna	Burnt umber	Viridian
Cobalt blue	Cerulean blue	Winsor blue	Payne's gray

overpainting effects

52

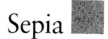
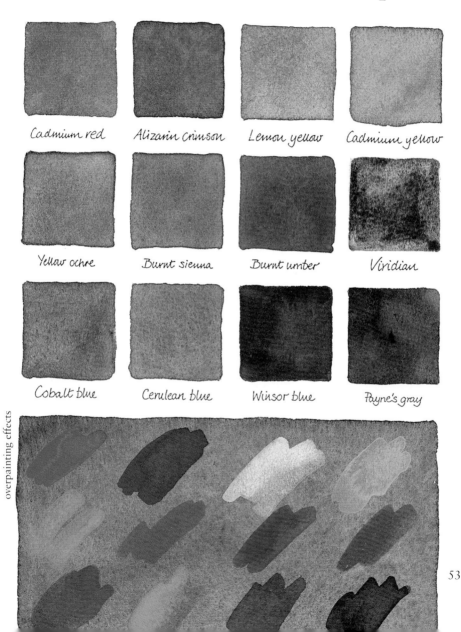

Cadmium red

Alizarin crimson

Lemon yellow

Cadmium yellow

Yellow ochre

Burnt sienna

Burnt umber

Viridian

Cobalt blue

Cerulean blue

Winsor blue

Payne's gray

overpainting effects

53

USING BROWNS AND BLUES

Red Flag Markers, Whitby
21ins × 28ins

THE GENTLE, nostalgic atmosphere is emphasized by the use of soft brown tones reminiscent of a sepia photograph. The artist has used washes of raw sienna in various strengths, and this, mixed with the other pigments, creates a muted palette which helps to unify the whole painting. The color has also been used for the surface of the water, reflecting the brown tones of the fishing boats and the quayside, and merging almost imperceptibly with the soft grays.

▼*The distant hills, disappearing into the mist, are painted with thin washes of cobalt and a drop of permanent rose. Cobalt was preferred to cerulean in this case as it is more transparent.*

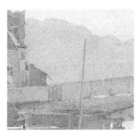

▶*A base wash of raw sienna has again been used for the whole quayside, with highlights overpainted with a cadmium yellow wash. The green mossy walls are mixes of raw sienna, cerulean and viridian, and the deep shadow areas are wet in wet applications of French ultramarine, used for its transparent quality.*

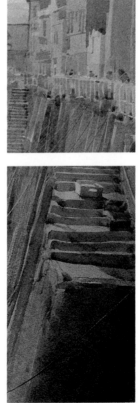

◀*The sunlit areas of the buildings are painted with mixed washes of raw sienna and permanent rose. Details and cool shadows are defined with thin washes of cobalt, while warmer details have touches of cadmium yellow.*

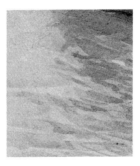

▲*To achieve the effect of shimmering water the artist used washes, some being worked wet in wet. They consist of mixes of cerulean, cobalt and raw sienna, with delicate touches of viridian and permanent rose.*

54

ARTIST David Curtis

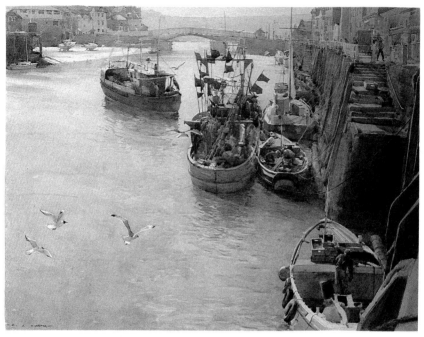

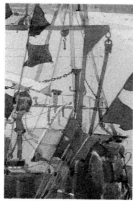

◀ *Even the red flags, which act as color highlights, are muted, the cadmium red being subdued by adding a small amount of raw sienna. White highlights sparkle throughout the whole painting. The artist used masking fluid to reserve small areas of white paper, a method which allows the washes to be applied freely.*

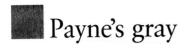 # Payne's gray

Cadmium red	Alizarin crimson
Lemon yellow	Cadmium yellow
Yellow ochre	Burnt sienna
Burnt umber	Viridian
Cobalt blue	Cerulean blue
Winsor blue	Payne's gray

overpainting effects

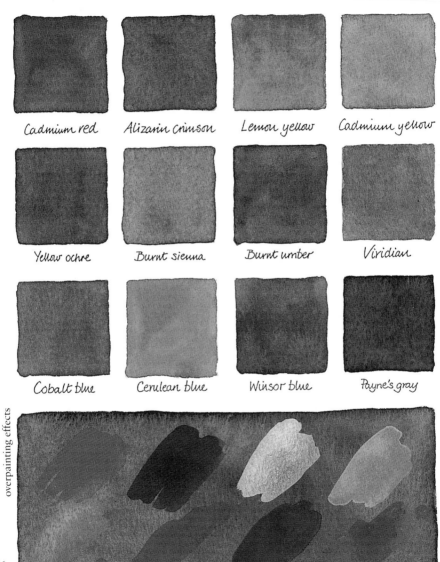

56

Davy's gray

Cadmium red	Alizarin crimson
Lemon yellow	Cadmium yellow
Yellow ochre	Burnt sienna
Burnt umber	Viridian
Cobalt blue	Cerulean blue
Winsor blue	Payne's gray

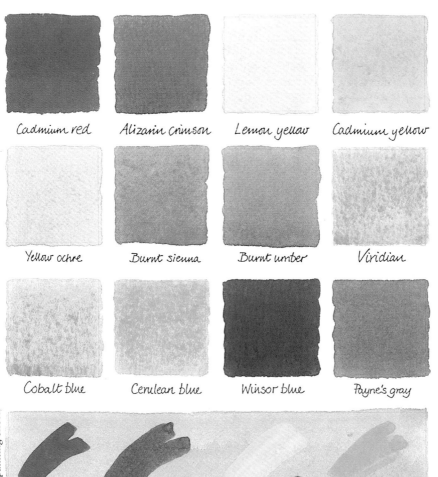

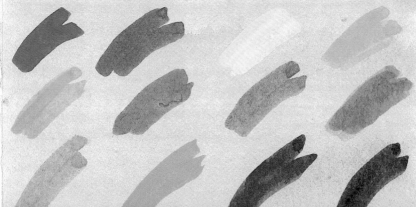

overpainting effects

57

MUTED COLORS

Fen Cottage
8ins × 12ins

THIS IS TAKEN from a sketchbook, and shows the art of mixing colors very clearly. The artist has used the actual page as a palette on which to mix and drop in the fluid colors. A very limited selection of colors was used to convey a dull winter's day. The cool colors — ultramarine, indigo and Paynes gray — and the spiky, linear pencil drawing emphasize the bleak atmosphere, but this is cleverly counterbalanced by thin washes and mixes of alizarin crimson and yellow ochre, giving the painting slight touches of warmth.

▷ *A thin dilution of yellow ochre formed the base color of the sky, with thin touches of ultramarine and crimson added to create variety.*

▽ *The basis of the whole painting can be seen in this detail: the artist has used various mixes of ultramarine, indigo, alizarin crimson and yellow ochre to create the desired cool and warm hues.*

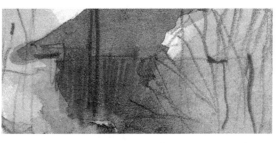

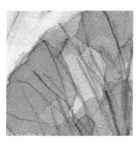

▲ *The skeleton drawing of the tree is given substance by washes of yellow ochre and ultramarine, with a little alizarin crimson for warmth.*

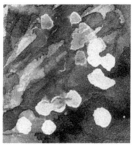

◁ *Dots and blobs of white gouache were used to depict the blossom on the leafless tree.*

ARTIST John Lidzey

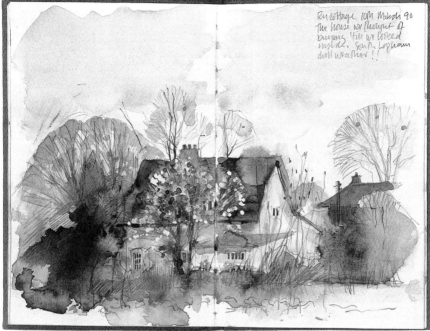

Fen Cottage 10th March 90
The house we thought of
buying 'till we looked
inside. South Lopham
dull weather!!

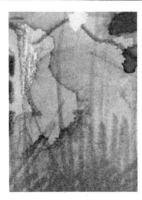

◄ *The subtle green hues
have been achieved by
mixes of aureolin yellow
and indigo.*

59

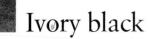

Ivory black

Ivory black is better than lamp black for mixtures as it is less dense.

Cadmium red	Alizarin crimson
Lemon yellow	Cadmium yellow
Yellow ochre	Burnt sienna
Burnt umber	Viridian
Cobalt blue	Cerulean blue
Winsor blue	Payne's gray

overpainting effects

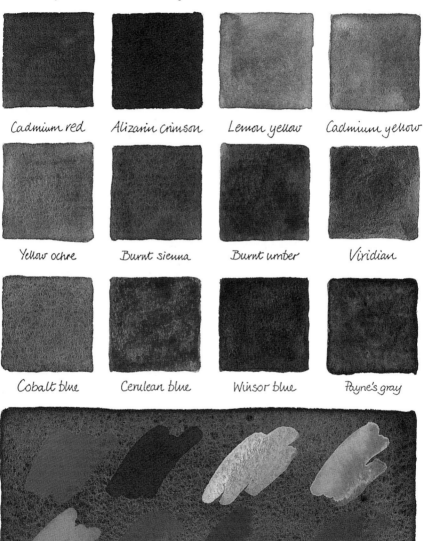

60

Chinese white

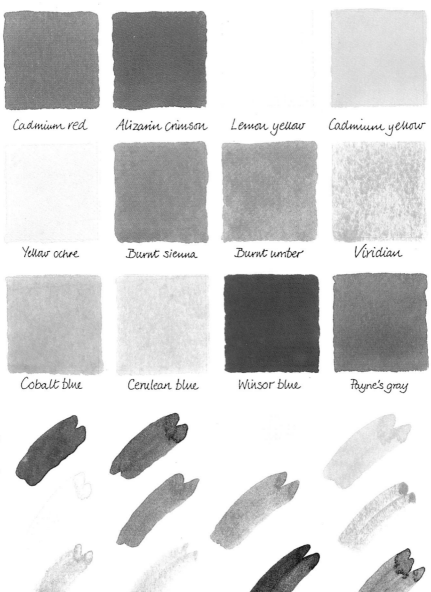

Cadmium red

Alizarin crimson

Lemon yellow

Cadmium yellow

Yellow ochre

Burnt sienna

Burnt umber

Viridian

Cobalt blue

Cerulean blue

Winsor blue

Payne's gray

overpainting effects

USEFUL MIXES: SKIN

SKIN TONES vary enormously: from one race to another, within the same racial group, from male to female, and even from one part of the body to another. The variety is made even wider by the light under which a particular person is seen, because skin will reflect light and also take on a certain amount of color from the surrounding hues. Thus the artist can use a whole range of colors, from yellow and reds in the highlights to blues, violets and greens in the shadows.

Experienced artists have their own favorite mixtures, but beginners often do not know where to start. These pages show five suggested skin-tone mixtures with highlights and shadows for each.

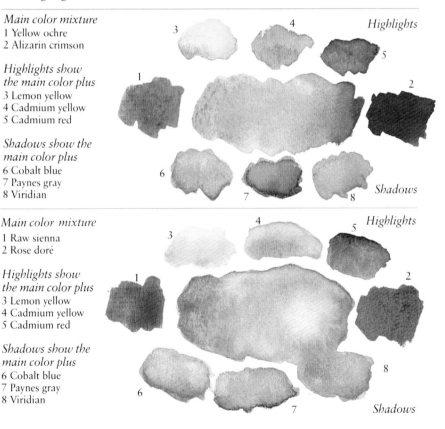

Main color mixture
1 Yellow ochre
2 Alizarin crimson

*Highlights show
the main color plus*
3 Lemon yellow
4 Cadmium yellow
5 Cadmium red

*Shadows show the
main color plus*
6 Cobalt blue
7 Paynes gray
8 Viridian

Highlights

Shadows

Main color mixture
1 Raw sienna
2 Rose doré

*Highlights show
the main color plus*
3 Lemon yellow
4 Cadmium yellow
5 Cadmium red

*Shadows show the
main color plus*
6 Cobalt blue
7 Paynes gray
8 Viridian

Highlights

Shadows

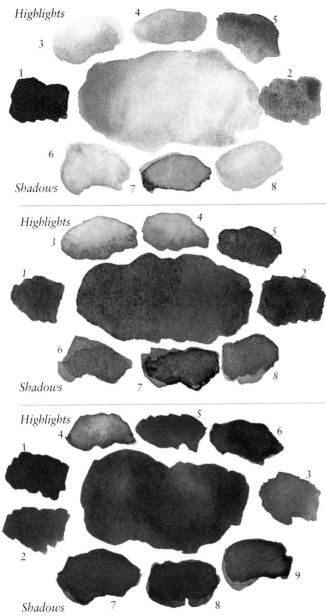

Highlights

3

1

4

5

2

6

7

8

Shadows

Main color mixture
1 Alizarin crimson
2 Raw sienna

Highlight mixtures
show main colour plus
3 Lemon yellow
4 Cadmium yellow
5 Cadmium red

Shadow mixtures show
main colour plus
6 Cobalt blue
7 Paynes gray
8 Viridian

Highlights

3

4

5

1

2

6

7

8

Shadows

Main color mixture
1 Cobalt blue
2 Burnt umber

Highlight mixtures
show main colour plus
3 Lemon yellow
4 Cadmium yellow
5 Cadmium red

Shadow mixtures show
main color plus
6 Cobalt blue
7 Paynes gray
8 Viridian

Highlights

5

4

6

1

3

2

7

8

9

Shadows

Main color mixture
1 Alizarin crimson
2 Sepia
3 Indigo

Highlight mixtures
show main color plus
4 Lemon yellow
5 Cadmium red

Shadow mixtures show
main color plus
7 Winsor violet
8 French
ultramarine
9 Viridian

63

CREDITS

CONTRIBUTING ARTISTS
16 Christopher Baker; 24 Moira Clinch; 34
Annie Williams (courtesy Canns Down
Press); 46 Moira Clinch; 54 David Curtis
(courtesy Richard Hagen, Broadway,
Worcestershire); 58 John Lidzey

Senior Editor
Hazel Harrison

Picture Research
Jane Lambert

Design Assistants
Penny Dawes
David Kemp
Kerry Davies

Color charts
Sally Launder
Moira Clinch

Typeset by QV Typesetting, London
Printed in Singapore by Star Standard Industries Pte Ltd